# A ROBIN'S HEART

## WILLIAM McDONALD

Book Design by: Aeyshaa
Cover by: Laird Atkins

ISBN: 979-8-9872043-0-6

# Table of Contents

# Chapter 1

As LouAnn looked at the clock in her room, she realized she had been watching TV all night. *Thank goodness I was able to finish my homework early so I could just relax.* She thought, after seeing it was getting very late.

As she was turning off the TV she happened to see a small brown bird staring in at her from the window sill. All of a sudden, another bird flew toward the brown bird as if to attack it. They both flew off. Not thinking anything of it, she rolled over and fell asleep almost instantly.

"It has been so much fun since our parents let us play and fly together," said Peanut, as the three friends flew on that bright sunny afternoon.

"I agree," responded Grace.

"Things have been ok for me too," said Joy, but Joy just didn't sound as happy as her two friends. So Peanut chirped "Are you ok, Joy? You haven't sounded like yourself lately."

"I'm fine, everything is great," Joy answered. But Peanut still didn't believe her. They were all having a nice afternoon and Peanut didn't want to upset everyone by pushing Joy.

Grace found a worm inching around the ground and alerted the others so they could have a good lunch. Peanut was the first to the ground and grabbed the worm in his beak so it wouldn't get away.

As the three finished eating, Joy said she had to leave. "I have some things to do, so I will see you guys tomorrow."

"OK" answered Grace and Peanut.

After Joy left, Peanut said, "Grace, does Joy sound OK to you? I have this feeling that something is wrong with her."

"She did seem a little strange today. I even noticed it yesterday too," answered Grace. The two friends had no idea what was bothering Joy. They figured it was probably nothing to worry about.

"So, twerp, I see you were with those other two know-nothings," said JJ, as Joy was flying back to her nest. "What do they see in a twerp like you?" JJ continued. "I can't believe any bird would want to hang out with you. I am surprised your parents don't throw you out of the nest."

"Just leave me alone JJ, and stop picking on me," said Joy. "Why do pick on me every day?" Joy asked as she started crying.

"Because it's fun. Besides, what are you going to do if I don't stop? You are so dumb and small, and even crying. What a baby you are! There is nothing you can do to stop me, so don't even try," replied JJ, laughing.

With that, Joy flew off as fast as she could just to get away from JJ. She knew she couldn't do anything to stop him no matter how much she wanted to. He was too ugly and she was very afraid of him. *I think he is a mockingbird,* she told herself.

"LouAnn, get up, it's time for school. You overslept again. I am getting tired of having to come up here every morning to get you up. You are 13 and are old enough that I shouldn't have to continually to treat you like you are a 2 year old. Now get up and get ready for school," yelled LouAnn's Mom as she turned the light on over LouAnn's bed. "Your breakfast will be ready in 10 minutes."

"Mom, turn off the light, it's too bright and hurts my eyes."

"Then get up, lazy" her mom yelled as she walked out of Lou Ann's room, slamming the door behind her.

LouAnn realized that she was dreaming about a bird named Joy who was being bullied. *Was Joy the brown bird at my window last night and as JJ the bird who flew toward the brown bird? Then again, it was only a dream, or was it?* Was LouAnn dreaming about what was happening to her every day at school? LouAnn knew there was something more to the dream. What was happening to Joy in her dream was not as bad as what was happening to her in real life.

Not only was she being teased about how ugly and how plain she looked, she was also being teased and bullied about how she was physically less mature than other girls in her class. If that wasn't enough, she was also receiving nasty text messages on her cell phone. Some of the boys in her class even texted her saying that she wasn't even good enough to post pictures of herself on any of the social media pages.

All this was going on without anyone at school or at home knowing about it. LouAnn kept this all to herself. She knew that if she said anything to her mom, her mom would tell her it was all in her mind and the kids at school really didn't mean anything by what they said or posted on social media. That it was just kids being kids. Besides all that, her mom was always yelling and screaming at her. LouAnn could not remember the last time her mom treated her nicely and not yelling and screaming.

LouAnn also knew that if she said anything to any of the teachers or counselors, they would either ignore her or tell her to get over it, that it was nothing and to grow up.

As LouAnn was getting ready for school, all she could think about was not going. She tried to think of some excuse to tell her mom so she didn't have to go and face those girls again. The only good thing was that today was Friday and she wouldn't see any of those girls over the weekend.

"Hurry up LouAnn, it's getting late and I have to get to work. I don't have time to wait around until you get good and ready to come down for breakfast," yelled her mother.

*Sure, Mom is even against me. She doesn't care about me, only herself,* thought LouAnn. *Maybe it would be better if I just weren't around. Then I wouldn't be a bother to anyone and the kids at school could pick on someone else.*

While LouAnn was getting ready, she was trying to think of how to get out of going to school. It was Friday, so maybe she could just skip school today and no one would miss her or even care that she wasn't there.

"Mom, I really don't feel that good today. I think I should stay home." LouAnn told her mom while having breakfast.

"You don't look sick. What's the matter, didn't you finish your homework, or do you have a test today that you didn't study for?" her mother asked.

*She just doesn't understand and she just doesn't care,* LouAnn said to herself. *I guess I just have to go.*

On the walk to school, all LouAnn could think about was trying to avoid the girls who kept on teasing and bullying her and the boys who kept on pointing at her laughing. Her only friend, Bonnie, didn't even go to the same school so she couldn't even see and talk to her today.

LouAnn no sooner got to school when she could sense some of the boys pointing and laughing at her. *Why can't they just leave me alone?* She thought. She was hoping she could get thru the day without any bullying and teasing.

That didn't last too long. During homeroom, she tried not to look around but she could see a couple of the new girls in school pointing at her and whispering. She wasn't sure what they were saying but, by the way two of the girls looked at her, she just knew they were whispering about her.

LouAnn no sooner walked into her English Lit class when she noticed a note being passed around. As each of the girls read the note, they looked up at her and snickered.

"Can't you all find someone else to bully and pick on? There is nothing about me that can be that interesting," said LouAnn before the teacher walked into the room.

*Well, I finally got through the morning, now all I have to do is get through lunch and my last 2 classes and I am home free,* she was thinking on her way to the cafeteria.

No such luck. "Hey you, who said you could eat here with the rest of us? You don't belong here. Why don't you go over into a corner where you belong? You are too ugly, too skinny, and you just don't belong," shouted Mattie, one of the girls who had been bullying and teasing her for months now. Everyone in the room turned to see what was going on. Some of the other kids were laughing and pointing and some just tried to ignore the whole scene, but no one stood up for her.

LouAnn just walked away and decided to sit outside by herself and eat her lunch.

The final bell rang, school was over for the weekend, and all LouAnn had to do was run out the door and get away from the bullies. Well, that didn't happen. One of the girls, from her last class, pulled on her backpack as she was walking down the hallway toward the exit. LouAnn lost her balance and fell backwards hitting the tiled floor hard.

"Look at LouAnn. She can't even walk without falling. You're so clumsy. Why don't you go home and ask your Mommy to teach you how to walk, or does she have walking problems too," said Mattie. All the other girls around them started laughing, which made LouAnn even more embarrassed. All she could do was pick herself up and hurry out the door and walk home, glad that it was Friday.

On the way home, LouAnn's cell phone pinged with the sound that she had a Twitter message. She stopped to open it. As soon as she saw it, she started crying. There was a picture of her laying on the hallway floor with the text "LouAnn can't even walk right #learntowalkugly."

With that, she ran home as fast as she could, unlocked the front door to her house, ran up to her room, and locked the door. She didn't want to talk to or see anyone. She was thankful it was Friday and she didn't have to see or deal with anyone all weekend.

"LouAnn, come on down for dinner before it gets cold. How many times do I have to call you to do something?" yelled her mom. "I'm not hungry," LouAnn shouted back. "I'm reading a book for school that I have to have done by Monday," which was a lie, but she couldn't come up with a better reason. What she was doing was sitting in the corner of her room on the floor, wishing she were dead.

Her mom did not push the issue. "When she gets hungry, she'll come down. I'm not going to baby her anymore," her mom told her dad. "I'm not going to pamper her either. She is 13 and old enough to know what she wants," she continued.

LouAnn continued sitting in the corner sobbing and wishing she were dead. *My mom doesn't even care about me, the kids at school bully me, and I have only one friend who I don't even see very often. No one would even miss me if I died,* she kept thinking. Before she knew it, it was after midnight. She turned on her laptop just to check her Instagram, Snapchat and Twitter pages. As soon as her Instagram page popped up, there it was another picture of her laying on the floor at school, with everyone standing around her. She realized it wasn't just a picture but a video. She pressed on the arrow and watched as she tried to get up and had problems. It even sounded like the kids who were standing all around her were laughing at her. The post with the video read, "LouAnn having problems walking. She can't even get up after falling. What a klutz she is!" Seeing and reading that, she started crying again. She slammed the screen on the laptop down and slid the computer across the floor to the other side the room.

It seemed she had been crying for hours before she finally fell asleep.

# *Chapter II*

As Joy flew away from JJ, she took a look back and saw JJ flying off in the opposite direction. She was very thankful that he wasn't following her.

Joy finally got back to her family nest, just hid in a corner of the nest, and cried herself to sleep. The next morning Joy told her parents she was flying off to play with her friends, but instead she flew off to be alone and think.

*Who can I tell about my problem?* she wondered? She couldn't think of anyone who could help her. That's when she decided to just stay hidden so that JJ couldn't find her.

"Thought you could hide from me, didn't you?" came a nasty voice from above. "But you aren't smart enough..., you're just too dumb of a bird!"

Joy looked up to see JJ peering meanly down at her from a higher branch. Her heart sank. Her plan to hide from the bully didn't worked.

JJ flew down and pulled on one of Joy's feathers with his big beak.

"Ouch! That hurt," shouted Joy. "You better not do that again, or I'll... I'll..."

"You'll do what? Tattle on me like a crybaby! Ha ha . . . there's more where that came from if you tell anyone!" JJ crowed.

Joy ruffled her feathers. She was scared. When JJ was sure that he had scared the little bird enough, he flew away.

Joy knew she had to tell someone, JJ was too mean and threatening for her to deal with alone, and hiding from him wasn't even working.

"Do you plan on sleeping all day, LouAnn? It's Saturday and you have chores to do around here," shouted her mom.

LouAnn rolled over and realized she had been sleeping on the floor all night. She looked at the clock and saw it was 10:17 in the morning already.

*Wow, I was dreaming again about that poor little bird named Joy who was being bullied, but why,* she thought? *Does this have anything to do with me being bullied? If a bird can't do anything about being bullied, why would I think I can do anything about it? Maybe I really am better off dead,* she continued thinking.

"Come on LouAnn, what are you doing up there? It's already after 10:30 and there's a lot to get done today" her mother shouted again. "You need to get your dirty clothes together and start the wash. You also need to clean your room and your bathroom. Then I want you to go shopping with me later."

*Oh great, she wants me to do all this stuff around the house, then go shopping with her,* LouAnn said to herself. *The last thing I want to do is go shopping, especially with my mother. I don't want to see or talk to anyone, today or any day. I don't know who is worse, my mom or the kids at school.*

LouAnn began picking up the clothes that were laying all over her room. She couldn't remember which were clean and which were dirty, so they all went into the wash. By the time she got her clothes together and into the wash machine, it was shortly before 1 PM and she was getting hungry.

*Maybe I can sneak downstairs and into the kitchen without mom seeing me,* she thought.

She was lucky, her mom was out in the yard watering the plants, so LouAnn was able to sneak into the kitchen, make a sandwich, get a drink and get back to her room before anyone saw her. She had no idea where her dad was or what he was doing, and she really didn't care, as long as no one saw her.

When she finished eating, it was time to tackle the rest of her room and put it back together again.

"Where's my computer," she said out loud, as if the computer would answer her. "I remember. I tossed it across the room last night. Oh, there it is under my desk." LouAnn put the computer back on her desk, thought about turning it on to see what was on Snapchat and Instagram. She didn't think about Twitter because, since the pictures were on Snapchat and

Instagram there was probably at least one on Twitter too, so why even check. Instead she decided to skip the computer and began making her bed and putting all her shoes away. As she was putting her shoes away, she heard the buzzer on the washer.

*Guess I need to put them in the dryer, no one else will,* she said to herself. Like any other typical teenager, all LouAnn's clothes went into the washer as one load, no separating of colors.

With that said, all the colors were now going into the dryer at the same time. "45 minutes should be plenty of time."

After putting all her clothes in the dryer, she decided to risk it and to check out her twitter page to see if there was anything new. She was hesitant to look because of what was posted yesterday after school. *Whew, nothing new from those nasty girls or boys since that post yesterday showing me on the floor at school.* She was relieved that they were leaving her alone for once.

"LouAnn, come on. It's time to go shopping. It's getting late and we need to get going," shouted her mom.

*Doesn't she do anything but shout at me? It would be so nice if mom would just come up and talk to me in a normal voice and not shout all the time.*

LouAnn decided to shout back — "I'm still cleaning my room and I still have the bathroom to clean and my clothes to fold and hang up. Then I still have to finish that book for school. Can't you go and handle it without me today? I really want to get all this done by tonight so I can relax tomorrow."

"Oh, OK, but I don't want you spending all day up there messing round. It would be nice if we saw you sometime today," yelled her mom.

"OK mom, I'll get it done as fast as I can," LouAnn lied.

LouAnn could hear the front door close and the car start. *Alone at last, no one to pester, nag or bully me. I still don't know where dad is, but he never pays much attention to me anyway, so who cares.*

LouAnn spent the rest of the afternoon finishing her room, folding all her clothes and cleaning her bathroom. By the time she was done, it was dinner time.

"Time for dinner, LouAnn," her mother shouted again.

"On my way," LouAnn shouted back. *Might as well get this over with, besides, I'm hungry,* she thought to herself.

"So, what book do you have to read for school?" LouAnn's mom asked during dinner.

"It's called <u>Night</u>. It's about the holocaust. Unbelievable what was done to the Jewish people during the Second World War. It is very hard reading because of all the horrible things that were done to them," LouAnn replied. *Wow, is mom really interested in what I am doing or is she just trying to get me to talk?* she thought to herself.

All LouAnn's dad did was turn toward the TV to see what the score of the football game was. He didn't seem interested in anything else. In fact LouAnn's mom didn't say anything else. *I guess mom really isn't interested in what I am doing,* LouAnn said to herself.

"Mom, dinner was great, but I still have homework to do and I'm not done with the book yet. I'm also tired from everything I had to do today. I am going to go back to my room now," LouAnn said to her mom as she was placing her dishes in the dishwasher.

Back in her room, all alone again. LouAnn began to wish she had friends who she could talk to about what was going on with her and the bullying at school.

There was only one girl who lived near her but went to a different school and didn't know what was going on in LouAnn's life. LouAnn didn't want to bother Bonnie with her problems, besides Bonnie wouldn't know what to do.

She opened her laptop to her Snapchat page and the first post she saw was another post about her. "LouAnn has no friends, she has no figure and is just a boring girl who is wasting everyone's time. She should just hide out for the rest of her life. She's such a loser." LouAnn had no idea who made the post, there was no name or picture attached.

*Can't they even leave me alone over the weekend? What have I ever done to them? I need to talk to someone about all this. The only person I can think of is Bonnie,* she thought. With those thoughts, LouAnn fell asleep.

# Chapter III

JJ flew down and pulled on one of Joy's feathers with his big beak.

"Ouch!" shouted Joy. "You better not do that again, or I'll... I'll...

"You'll do what? Tattle on me like a crybaby? Ha ha . . . there's more where that came from if you tell anyone!" JJ crowed.

Joy ruffled her feathers. She was scared. When JJ was sure that he had scared the little bird, he flew away.

Joy knew she had to tell someone. JJ was too mean and threatening for her to deal with alone—and hiding from him wasn't even working.

*Why am I dreaming this again? I just had this dream last night. What are they trying to tell me?* Lou Ann said to herself after this dream woke her up. She looked at her clock and noticed it was only 2:36 in the morning. *I don't know why I keep dreaming about this bird getting bullied. If this little bird can't hide or find a way to solve her problem, how am I supposed to solve mine?* With that LouAnn fell back to sleep.

"But who?" Suddenly, Joy thought of Hopper, the wise old painted bunting who had helped free Grace from a trap and convinced their parents to let them all play together.

"I know he is brave enough to help me. Now I just have to find him . . . and fast. Peanut and Grace will know where he is!" she said out loud.

"I need Mr. Hopper's help!" Joy said, landing beside Peanut and Grace on an old, broken weathervane.

"Why," both Peanut and Grace said at the same time. "Tell us everything," glad that Joy was finally asking for help.

Joy told them about JJ. They weren't surprised that the mockingbird was up to his nasty tricks.

"All the birds fly away from him because he is so mean!" Peanut said. "Why didn't you tell us he was bullying you?"

"I didn't want you to think I couldn't take care of myself," answered Joy. Being bullied was embarrassing.

With that, Lou Ann heard her mother shouting yet again.

"LouAnn, it's time to get up and get ready for church. We have to leave in 30 minutes, so get a move on." *There she goes again, shouting at me. Can't she ever just talk to me in a normal voice and not shout and scream all the time,* LouAnn said to herself.

*Again, with that bird dream. I still don't understand why I am having these dreams all the time,* Lou Ann was thinking as she was getting out of bed. *I am tired of this continuing saga about a bird being bullied. It's like I'm watching a long running TV show, but instead of me being the lead character in the series, it's a bird,* she kept thinking as she was getting ready for church.

Church was uneventful. No one from her school went to the church her and her parents went to. The only one she knew was Bonnie. LouAnn and Bonnie talked for a few minutes after the service ended, but LouAnn said nothing about being bullied. All she told Bonnie was about the crazy dreams was having about a bird being bullied and picked on. She asked Bonnie, if Bonnie had any idea why she was having these dreams.

Bonnie's first question was "Is anything like that happening to you? Many times, when people dream, the dreams are a reflection of something that is happening in real life." "No, not me," answered LouAnn.

"Then, do you know anyone at your school or neighborhood that is being bullied?" asked Bonnie.

"Nope, not a clue," LouAnn lied. "I have no idea why this is happening."

"LouAnn, let's go, we have to go home," yelled her mother.

"Ok, see you soon. Let me know what happens to that bird of yours if you have the dream again," said Bonnie, as she walked away.

"Bye. I'll call you in a day or two," LouAnn replied. "So, how is Bonnie doing? You haven't seen her in a while. What is she up to?" asked LouAnn's mom, during their drive home.

"She's ok. We didn't have that much time to talk. I told her I would call her in a day or two to catch up on things," answered LouAnn.

The rest of the day was very quiet. LouAnn spent the time in her room, doing a little studying, but mostly enjoying doing nothing and not being bothered by anyone. She didn't even open her laptop or check her phone. All she wanted to do was relax and watch TV. She found a romantic comedy movie and just laid back on her bed and watched the movie.

"LouAnn, it's time for dinner. Hurry up before it gets cold," yelled her mom.

What perfect timing, the movie had just ended about 10 minutes before. *There she goes again, yelling for no reason,* LouAnn thought, as she headed downstairs.

"Have you finished that book you told me about the other night?" asked her Mom.

*Wow, Mom is asking me about the book. Is she interested or does she just want to know what I am doing?* LouAnn thought. "Yes, I finished it and just about finished the report. I just have a little more to do," she answered.

There was no response from her mother. As usual, her dad kept turning around, checking the TV to see what was happening with his favorite football team. "Did you say something, LouAnn?" asked her dad, during a commercial.

"I just told mom that I am almost finished with my report on the book <u>Night</u>" said LouAnn.

"Oh, ok," replied her dad as he turned back to the TV.

The rest of the dinner and dessert went without any more talking.

After dinner, LouAnn went outside to fill her bird feeder with seeds. As she held her hand out to put some seeds in the bird feeder, a tiny very colorful bird flew down and landed in the palm of her hand. He eats a few seeds, then cocks his head while looking at her and off he flies.

LouAnn finished filling the bird feeder and headed back to her room to watch some more TV, falling asleep during the movie she was watching.

# Chapter IV

"**I** need Mr. Hopper's help!" Joy said, landing beside Peanut and Grace on an old broken weathervane.

"Tell us everything," her friends said, glad that Joy was finally asking for help.

Joy told them about JJ. They weren't surprised that the mockingbird was up to his nasty tricks.

"All the birds fly away from him because he is so mean!" Peanut said. "Why didn't you tell us he was bullying you?"

"I didn't want you to think I couldn't take care of myself," answered Joy. Being bullied was embarrassing.

Grace cut in, "But we're friends, Joy. Friends help each other. When I got into trouble, you guys helped me. I felt dumb because I couldn't tell the difference between a rope and a worm. You helped set me free. If it weren't for you two, I wouldn't be here today."

Joy spread her wings and wrapped them around her two friends. She felt good to have them as friends.

"Let's go find Mr. Hopper," Peanut said.

"I saw him heading toward the old red bam in the farmer's field this morning," Grace told her friends. "Let's check if he's still there."

Off the trio flew to the old red bam.

There, high in the rafters, sat Hopper.

"We need your help again Sir," explained Peanut.

Joy told the old painted bunting all the nasty things JJ had been saying and doing. Grace chimed in that, all season long, JJ had been bullying other birds, too. They had all learned to stay far away from him.

"I think I know how to help," said Hopper after hearing their side of the story. "I need to talk to JJ to hear what he has to say."

Joy flapped her wings. "No! That will only make things worse. He told me not to tell anyone!"

"The last time I helped you fledglings, everything turned out for the best, so please trust me.

And just like the time before, Hopper was off and out of the barn before the three friends could say anything else.

*Here we go again. Another night with those birds, but WHY?* thought LouAnn as her alarm clock rang. *At least it isn't a repeat from the other night,* she thought.

As LouAnn was getting ready for school, all she could think about was the bullying she would get again all day at school.

*"I have to do something. I need to talk to someone, but who?"* she kept saying to herself as she headed downstairs for breakfast.

"Did you FINALLY finish that report for school?" her mother asked in a sarcastic voice.

"Yes, I did," answered LouAnn. *Again, mom can't just ask me nicely, she had to be sarcastic in the way she talked to me.* "LouAnn thought.

Before heading off to school, LouAnn had to check the bird feeder and add some bird seeds to make sure it was full for the day. As she was finishing, she still had some seeds in her hand. Before she could put the seeds back in the bag, the small, multi colored bird landed in the palm of her hand again. He ate a couple of seeds, cocked his head as he looked at her and then flew off.

All the way to school, all she could think about was the dream she kept on having about the poor little bird who was being bullied and picked on. What was this dream trying to tell her? Did she finally need to talk to someone who might be able to help her, but who? Also, what was the connection with that strange multi colored bird this morning and the way he looked at me? *Was that bird supposed to be Hopper, the multi colored bird in my dreams?* She wondered.

When she finally got to school, she got a big surprise. There, standing at the front entrance was her friend Bonnie.

"Surprise," said Bonnie.

With a look of surprise and shock on her face, LouAnn said, "What are you doing here? You don't go to this school?"

"I do now. My parents talked to me about transferring to this school. It is closer to our house and after they did some research on this school, they said it was a better school for me, so here I am." answered Bonnie.

Still having that surprised look on her face, LouAnn said, "Did you know about this yesterday, why didn't you tell me, when did they transfer you?"

"Slow down," said Bonnie. "Yes, I knew about it yesterday, but wanted to surprise you. That's why I didn't tell you yesterday. The Transfer came thru this past Friday, so today is my first day. By the look on your face, you seem to be in shock and surprised."

"I am. Just cannot believe you are here, going to the same school," answered LouAnn. *Great, now, my only friend is going to see that I am getting bullied. Now I cannot hide it anymore from her.* Thought LouAnn.

The girls heard the bell ringing. "Well, hope to see you at lunch. Good luck," said LouAnn.

"Thanks, see you then," replied Bonnie.

And off they went to their classes.

*How am I going to tell Bonnie about being bullied? She will see it at lunch when the girls start in on me. Maybe I can just avoid seeing Bonnie during lunch and catch up with her after school,* LouAnn was thinking on her way to homeroom.

As LouAnn was entering the cafeteria for lunch, she saw Bonnie standing at the entrance waiting on her.

"Here comes that ugly, shapeless, waste of a person again," shouted one of LouAnn's bullies.

When the bully heard Bonnie talking to LouAnn, she turned to Bonnie and said, "I don't know who you are but if I were you, I wouldn't waste my time talking to this ugly girl," pointing to LouAnn. "As you can see, she is ugly, has no figure, and just a boring twerp."

*Wow, this girl just used the same word about me that JJ, the bully, said to Joy, in my dreams. I wonder if all bullies think alike,* thought LouAnn.

"I don't appreciate you talking to and about my friend like that. I'm sure she has done nothing to you or your friends, so just leave her alone," replied Bonnie.

With that the bullies walked away leaving Bonnie and LouAnn alone.

"What was that all about?" said Bonnie. "I thought you told me everything was good at school. You even told me yesterday when you told me about your dreams that you were not experiencing any of what you were dreaming about. I thought you were my friend. You know you can tell me anything."

Looking sad and staring at the floor, LouAnn realized she finally had to say something to Bonnie about being bullied. "I was afraid you would think that I couldn't handle any of this by myself. I thought you would think less of me if I said anything."

"What? We have known each other for a long time and you have helped me in the past. Why would you ever think that I would think less of you or think you couldn't deal with it," answered Bonnie. "The question now is, what are we going to do about it? I have an idea. I know a teacher from my old school who does subbing here at this school sometimes. I think we should go talk to her and see if she has any ideas that will help you."

LouAnn smiled a little, "OK, I'm willing to go and see what she has to say."

"OK then. I know she stays after school most of the time, so tomorrow after school we will hop on the bus and go see her." Bonnie said with a smile.

# Chapter V

As LouAnn fell asleep that night she was feeling much better that she finally told Bonnie about being bullied. It seemed like a big weight was lifted off her shoulders. The only thing she could think about now was, what could this teacher tell her that would help?

Joy told the old painted bunting all the nasty things JJ was saying and doing to her. Grace chimed in that, JJ had been bullying other birds too. They had all learned to stay away from him.

"I think I know how to help," said Hopper after hearing their side of the story. "I need to talk to JJ to hear what he has to say."

Joy flapped her wings. "NO! That will only make things worse. He told me not to tell anyone."

"The last time I helped you fledglings, everything turned out for the best, didn't it? So, please trust me again this time."

LouAnn jumped out of bed in a panic. *What if this teacher wants to go talk to Mattie and the other girls just like the bird did in my dreams? I have to tell Bonnie that it's a bad idea to go and talk to that teacher.* With that thought, LouAnn laid back down in her bed and, after a short time, fall back to sleep.

She didn't dream the rest of the night.

LouAnn was waiting for Bonnie at the front of the school before classes started. She wanted to tell Bonnie that it was a bad idea to talk to the teacher this afternoon.

"I am afraid that if we tell the teacher friend of yours after school today, she might talk to some of the teachers or principal the next time she subs here and that will cause even more problems for me. The teachers or principal here might punish everyone who is bullying me and then they will come after me even worse than they are now," said LouAnn, in a worried voice.

Bonnie just smiled as said, "Trust me. I know this teacher well enough to know she would not do anything like that. We are going to go right after school and that's final." As soon as the last bell rang, Bonnie and LouAnn hopped on the bus and headed over to Bonnie's old school. They went straight to the classroom Bonnie knew the teacher would be in.

"Wow, this is a surprise Bonnie. I didn't ever expect to see you again after you transferred to the new school the other day. What brings you back here?" Said Bonnie's old teacher.

"Hi Miss Maysfield. This is my friend LouAnn. She has a problem and you were the first person I thought of who might be able to help her," replied Bonnie.

"Well, nice to meet you LouAnn. Bonnie has told me about you, so I feel I know a lot about you already. What kind of problem are you having? Does it have anything to do with one of your subjects at school?" Asked Miss Maysfield.

LouAnn, looking sad and staring at the floor, started to talk, "No, my problem has nothing to do with any of my subjects, in fact I am getting really good grades in all my subjects. My problem has to do with the fact that I am being teased and bullied by some of the girls in my school. They say that I am ugly and have no figure. That I should stay at home and hide. They have even taken pictures and videos and posted them on social media pages. They even have the boys teasing me about how ugly and plain I look. It is so bad that I don't even want to go to school anymore. I have even wondered if it would be much better for everyone if I were dead."

Bonnie jumped in, "I saw it yesterday at lunch. The girls wouldn't leave her alone. They even made negative comments to me about why would I even bother to be a friend to someone like LouAnn. That I should just walk away and leave and have nothing to do with her."

"First off, I don't want you to even think about killing yourself. Get that thought out of your head immediately. I can get you help if you are seriously thinking that. As for the rest, I understand exactly what you girls are talking about. When I was a young girl, a little older than you, in high school, I was just like you. I was, what they called, a late bloomer. That is someone who develops later than most girls and boys. I would be teased all the time. When I went shopping with some of the girls from school, they would go look a fancy bras and tell me to go look someplace else because I didn't need to be in that section of the store. As you can see, I did develop and the teasing stopped. At that time, we didn't call it bullying, just teasing, but it hurt just the same. I have to go sub at your school this Friday, so I should probably talk to one of your teachers about this. The reason being is that since I don't officially work at your school full time, it would be improper for me to talk to those girls," said Miss Maysfield.

LouAnn had that panic look on her face again. "NO! That will only make things worse. Can I tell you about this dream I have been having for the past couple of weeks. In fact, it is a continuing dream each night. What I have been dreaming is what is happening right now."

With that, LouAnn told Miss Maysfield all about her dreams of a robin named Joy who was being bullied by a mockingbird named JJ.

When she finished, Miss Maysfield smiled and asked how the dream ended.

"I don't know. The dream has only gotten to the point where the painted bunting, named Hopper, flew off to talk to JJ. Just like you want to do Friday when you come to our school," answered LouAnn.

"I understand your concern, but please, trust me. Now, both of you, go enjoy the rest of the week and I will let you know what I plan on doing when I see you both on Friday," Miss Maysfield said as she got up and helped them to the door.

As they were leaving LouAnn turned to Bonnie, "I only hope Miss Maysfield doesn't make things worse and, for the first time, I want to continue this dream of mine to see what happens to the bird."

The rest of the week was the same, LouAnn was being bullied every day and even Bonnie was getting teased for being a friend of LouAnn's.

LouAnn's dream of the birds just kept repeating and repeating. Each night her dream would end with Hopper telling the birds to trust him and flying off to talk to JJ.

*What is going on? Why can't this dream end? What happens when Hopper talks to JJ?* LouAnn kept on asking herself each morning when she woke up.

Finally Friday morning arrived. "LouAnn, you haven't told me how your dream about the birds ended," said Bonnie, as she met LouAnn at the front of the school.

Looking upset, LouAnn said, "It hasn't, every night I kept repeating the same part of the dream. Hopper would tell the birds he had to talk to JJ and that the birds should trust him as they had before. That is where it stops every night. I wish it would end. I am really getting tired of having the same thing happen every night."

"Well today is the day that Miss Maysfield is going to tell us who she talked to about all this. Maybe everything will change after school today," replied Bonnie. "I have to get to class, see you at lunch."

As the day progressed, it was just like any other day, more bullying and teasing.

When the final bell rang, Miss Maysfield was waiting outside the door of LouAnn's classroom.

"Hi Miss Maysfield," said LouAnn, as she exited the classroom. "Did you talk to  the girls or any of the teachers?"

"Yes I did. I talked to Miss Spaulding. She knows the girls because they are in one of her classes. I understand that you are also in one of her classes, but not the same one the girls are in, correct? She is getting the girls together and taking them to the cafeteria to talk with them," said Miss Maysfield.

"Yes, I have Miss Spaulding for my English Lit class," answered LouAnn.

At the same time, Miss Spaulding was waiting outside the classroom of the girls who were bullying LouAnn.

"Hi girls. Do you have a few minutes, I would like to talk to you down in the cafeteria," Said Miss Spaulding.

"OK. We don't have to go home right away, so we have a few minutes to talk. Is there a problems with our grades? We thought we were doing okay in your class." they asked as they got to the cafeteria.

"No, it has nothing to do with your grades," answered Miss Spaulding.

Walking into the cafeteria, "I need to talk to you about LouAnn and how you have been treating her," continued Miss Spaulding.

"That little twerp. Wait until I get my hands on her. We told her not to talk to or tell anyone or we would make things even worse for her," the girls all said in almost the same tone.

Miss Spaulding stopped them right there. "That's what I am talking about. Why are you being so mean and hurtful to LouAnn and her friend, Bonnie? What did they ever do to you for you to be so mean to them?"

"Have you seen her? She is so plain. She has no figure, never wears makeup and doesn't even wear the nicest clothes like the rest of us. She wants to be friends but how can we be friends when she looks like that? We have even noticed that all her teachers like her and treat her better than us or anyone else. Why can't the teachers treat us as nice?" The girls said.

Miss Spaulding sat quietly and just listened as the girls talked and talked.

When the girls finished talking, Miss Spaulding sat up, thought for minute and then said, "The first thing you all need to know is that before you can except others to like or love you, you must first like and love yourself. If you cannot do that, then how can you expect others to like and/or love you? You know girls, people aren't all the same. Maybe LouAnn doesn't know about putting makeup on. Maybe her parents work so hard to take care of her and her family that they don't have time to take her places, buy her newer clothes or teach her things. As for her figure, every girl develops at a different speed. When I was young, I didn't start developing until I was 15. I got teased every day. Other kids would even tell me that I didn't have to worry about getting any bras because all I needed were boys t shirts. Then one morning I woke up and I began developing. It got to the point that many of the girls envied me. They stopped teasing me and wanted to be my friends. So, you see, people change. Looking at me today, you would never know or believe what I looked like and went through back when I was in school."

"Now, I want you all to leave LouAnn and Bonnie alone all weekend and Monday. Tell the boys too. No text messages, Snapchat, Instagram posts, tweets, etc. No contact with them until we meet again Monday after school right here," Miss Spaulding said. "Ok, now you girls can leave and have a wonderful weekend."

With that said, the girls left. Miss Spaulding could hear them talking to each other and looking back at her.

"We saw the girls leaving just now and they didn't even look at us. They kept walking and talking to each other. We even saw them talking to a couple of boys on the other side of the fence. No-one even looked our way," said Bonnie. Even LouAnn looked confused and wondered why the girls didn't say anything.

"Let's go see what Miss Spaulding said to them," said Bonnie as she started back into the school.

All Miss Spaulding said was that she would see LouAnn and Bonnie in the cafeteria Monday afternoon after school. With that said, Miss Spaulding left the school and LouAnn and Bonnie headed to LouAnn's house. Bonnie was spending the weekend at LouAnn's. They were having a sleepover.

# Chapter VI

"Let's talk," Hopper said, landing next to JJ on a tree branch.

"Who do you think you are, old bird?" said JJ with a scowl. "You're old and small, and you don't have anything interesting to say to me!"

The colorful bird didn't let the bully's words bother him. "Why are you so mean and nasty to all the other birds, but especially to Joy?" Hopper asked gently.

"That little twerp told on me? I'll get even with her," JJ replied and tried to take off.

But Hopper held him back with a touch of his wing. The mockingbird might be bigger, but Hopper had enough courage for a whole flock.

"Oh no you won't," he said sternly. "Please tell me what's wrong. Why aren't you able to treat the other birds so kindly?"

"You wouldn't understand," JJ said, looking sad. "I'm not small or colorful like the others. I'm big, gray, ugly and scary. I know the other birds say mean things about me behind my back. So I pick on them because . . . well, because they have friends, and I don't." JJ hung his head.

"So you're jealous of their friendships?" Hopper asked. He knew JJ was good at heart. He just had to show JJ that his size didn't frighten him. "Why do you think they talk about you?"

JJ shrugged his wings, and Hopper explained, "Because you are mean to them and sometimes you even hurt them. It's not because of how you look, JJ."

The mockingbird started to look interested, and Hopper felt hopeful.

The wise bird continued, "Different birds have different looks: Some are blue, some red, some brown, some yellow, and some are even gray and white like you. Look at me. I am multicolored. When I was young, I was a dull green before my colors came in, and the older birds teased me. But I soon learned that it's more important what's inside of me than what's on the outside. The *real* you, JJ, is on the inside, too."

JJ thought about that for a moment, then asked, "How can I show others the real me when all the birds fly away from me? I won't be able to get close enough to let them know I'd rather be friends than be a bully."

"I will give you a hand. You can trust me," replied Hopper. "Meet me at the old red barn tomorrow morning." With that, Hopper flew off.

"LouAnn, wake up," said Bonnie.

LouAnn, looking strange, opened her eyes, looked at Bonnie and said, "What's wrong?"

I was having the dream again about the birds, but this time, the bird named Hopper was talking to the bully and found out why JJ was being a bully."

"You had this very strange look on your face. I thought something was wrong," replied Bonnie.

"No, I'm ok. I was just surprised to find out why the mockingbird was being a bully. I think I will have another dream because Hopper told JJ to meet him in the old red barn the next day. As you woke me, I was thinking that Miss Spaulding wanted to see us Monday after school in the cafeteria. Remember? I am really beginning to understand that I am having this continuing dream because it is happening to me just like in the dream," continued LouAnn.

"If you are right about you living the dream, do you think Miss Spaulding found out why the girls are bullying you? I wonder if she is going to tell us on Monday why you are being bullied," said Bonnie.

LouAnn continued, "I thought about that too, but right now I just want to have fun this weekend. Remember, Miss Spaulding said she told the girls not to contact us at all this weekend, not even on any of our social media accounts. She said she even told the girls to tell the boys to leave us alone. Maybe that's what the girls were telling the boys when we saw them talking thru the fence yesterday. So, I just want us to enjoy this weekend and not think about the birds or the girls or anything like that."

"OK then, what do you want to do? My mom said I could stay here until tomorrow night. I'm getting hungry, so let's get dressed and have some breakfast," said Bonnie as you could hear her stomach grumble a little.

As the girls headed downstairs, they could smell bacon frying.

"Good morning girls. Breakfast will be ready in a couple of minutes. I have the bacon frying and just getting ready to put the pancakes on. Hope you are both hungry," said Mrs. Richeson.

LouAnn looked a little surprised and was thinking. *Wow, mom is being very friendly this morning. Wonder what changed. Oh, I bet it's just because Bonnie is here.*

As LouAnn's mom was placing the pancakes and bacon in front of the girls, she asked, "Do you girls have any special plans for the day? I was thinking of going to mall and wanted to know if you would like to join me. We could go and just set a time to meet up to have lunch in the food court or come home to eat. What do you think of that idea?" *Is this really my mom? I cannot believe how she is acting, but I really like it,* thought LouAnn. Looking at LouAnn, Bonnie said, "That sounds like a lot of fun. We could go around to the different stores and check out the clothes and makeup. Maybe we could even go to one of the stores and see if we could get a makeover. I know that sometimes the make-up counters have women who will give free makeovers."

"Sure, why not. It's something different and does sound like fun," replied LouAnn.

"OK then, you girls go on back upstairs and finish getting ready while I clear the table and start the dishwasher," said Mrs. Richeson.

As luck would have it, there was a new make-up store in the mall that was offering make-overs free of charge.

"Can you believe it? Just what we were talking about at breakfast, free makeovers," said Bonnie excitedly.

LouAnn wasn't too sure. "I normally don't wear makeup so I have no idea how I would look or if I would even like it."

"So, it's free. If you don't like it, you can always go into one of ladies restrooms and take it off," exclaimed Bonnie.

"OK, I'll give it a try," replied LouAnn.

"Good morning ladies. Would you both like to try one of our makeovers? They are free for today only," said the makeup artist.

Bonnie was the first to answer, "Yes we both would like makeovers. I have to let you know that my friend here doesn't ever wear makeup so this will be a totally new experience for her."

"No problem. We have had a few ladies in this morning who have never worn makeup.

I will work on your friend and my partner will do your makeup. By the way, my name is Kali and this is my partner, Jessica. Any questions before we start?" Asked Kali.

LouAnn and Bonnie sat in chairs and let Kali and Jessica work on the girls' makeup.

Just as Kali and Jessica were finishing up, LouAnn's mom happened to walk by and noticed the girls were getting makeovers.

"Wow, I cannot believe my eyes. You girls look absolutely beautiful. LouAnn, I have never seen you look so pretty before. If you like what this lady has done, I will buy you whatever makeup she suggests," said LouAnn's mom smiling.

Kali and Jessica finished the girls' makeover and handed them mirrors so they could see what was done.

Bonnie looked at LouAnn and couldn't believe her eyes. "LouAnn, you are beautiful. I can't believe you never wanted to wear makeup before. Look in your mirror."

With that, LouAnn looked into her mirror at what Kali was able to do. Not too much but not too little. Just enough to have a major effect on how LouAnn looked. "Is this really me? I really like it. I didn't think I would. I was very nervous, but I love it. Mom, if you don't mind, I really would like it if you bought me some of what Kali just applied on me."

Looking very happy, LouAnn's mom said, "of course I will buy it for you. You look so beautiful. I think you should start wearing makeup every day. What does everyone else think?"

All three of the others agreed. Kali had done fantastic job.

As they left the store, after buying makeup for both LouAnn and Bonnie, LouAnn whispered to Bonnie, "I really like it and will not go to the ladies restroom to wash it off."

"Alright girls, lunch time. So let's head to the food court. You pick what you want to eat and lunch is on me," said Mrs. Richeson.

The rest of the day was just window shopping and trying on various outfits in different stores.

It was getting a little late in the day, so they all decided to go back home and have a relaxing evening.

# Chapter VII

After dinner, LouAnn decided to check her social media accounts. Nothing. No comments or nasty posts from anyone. The day was ending as the best day of her young life.

Later that night LouAnn had a hard time falling asleep. All she could think about was what a great day they all had. She was even surprised on how pleasant and nice her mother was all day.

As she was finally falling asleep, she wondered if she would still have the dream about the birds.

The day was so perfect, she didn't want to ruin it with the bullying dream.

The next day, Hopper found the three friends perched on a low branch in a maple tree.

"Mr. Hopper, did you talk JJ into leaving me alone?" Joy asked hopefully.

"Well, I did talk to JJ," Hopper said, "but I didn't ask him to leave you alone . . . not exactly. There are things about JJ you don't know. He is insecure about how he looks. He thinks everyone is afraid of him because he is so large and ugly. He could benefit from friends who don't judge him by how he looks."

The three young birds started chirping all at once, but Hopper whistled to get their attention. "He wants to apologize and show you who he really is ... on the inside. Are you ready to hear him out?"

"But he said so many nasty things and even pulled my feathers. How can I forgive him for that?" Joy exclaimed.

The dream startled LouAnn awake. She looked at the clock and saw it was only 6:30. *Too early to get up but I am wide awake now. Maybe if I just lay here, I can fall back asleep.*

She must have finally fallen back asleep because when she look at the clock again, it was 8:17.

Bonnie was just rolling over and as she opened her eyes, she was surprised to see LouAnn already awake.

"Wants wrong, you look a little upset." Asked Bonnie.

"Yea, I am. I had that dream again and it startled me. Apparently this bird Hopper not only talked to JJ, the bully, but had him come to the red barn and then Hopper told the other birds too so they could all talk. It made me think that Miss Spaulding may be doing the same thing to us tomorrow after school. I think she is going to have all of us meet and talk to each other. I don't think I am ready to do that. After all, they have been very mean and nasty and even tried to hurt me by making me trip and fall," said LouAnn.

Looking straight into LouAnn's eyes, Bonnie replied... "Look, we had a wonderful, fun day yesterday, just the two of us and at times even with your mom. Let's not let this dream of yours ruin today. We have no idea what will happen tomorrow after school, so there is no need to spend today worrying about it. You are my best friend and I will not allow you to let this get you down. So, let's get up, put something on and see what your mom has for us this morning."

With that, the girls threw on some clean clothes and headed downstairs to see what LouAnn's mom was making this morning for breakfast.

As they got to the bottom of the stairs, they could hear crackling coming from the kitchen. Turning to LouAnn, Bonnie said, "That sounds and smells like sausages frying. I love sausages."

Hearing the girls enter the kitchen LouAnn's mom said good morning, without even turning around to see them.

"Mom, those sausages smell delicious. What are we having with it?" Asked LouAnn. Turning around this time, LouAnn's mom said, "Well, I thought it would be nice if we had sausages, toast and eggs any way you like it. LouAnn, I know you like scrabbled eggs with cheese. How about you Bonnie, how do you like your eggs cooked?"

Bonnie replied, "I never had them scrabbled with cheese, so that sounds like something I would like to try."

"Ok then, sausages, toast and scrambled eggs with cheese it is. Have a seat girls. It will be ready in a couple of minutes. Drink your orange juice in the meantime. There is always more if you want some more," said Mrs. Richeson as she started on the eggs. Do you girls have anything planned for today? If not, the community pool is still open if you both want to go swimming."

"Oh, I don't know. I think we might just hang out around here and see about putting on some of that makeup you bought us yesterday. This way I can get it right before school tomorrow," LouAnn replied.

Bonnie nodded as if to say that it was a good idea.

"OK, if you girls need any help with your makeup, just give me a shout and I will be right up to see what I can do to help you," Mrs. Richeson said between bites of her toast.

When the girls got back to LouAnn's room, Bonnie commented, "I really like your mom. She is so nice and friendly and kind. It must be great having a mom like that. I wish my mom was that nice to me."

LouAnn looked surprised, "What we are seeing this weekend is not what my mom is normally like. I don't know what has come over her, but normally she is screaming and yelling at me all the time, from the time I get up until after dinner when I come back up here to finish my homework or just watch TV. I hope to talk to her and tell how much I appreciate the way she has been this weekend."

The rest of the day was pretty much uneventful. The girls practiced putting on and taking off their makeup. At one point LouAnn's mom came up to see if the girls needed any help and gave them some pointers on easier ways to put on and take off their makeup.

Before they knew it, it was time for dinner. LouAnn's dad was outside grilling burgers for all of them. Even that surprised LouAnn.

After a dinner of burgers, French fires and salads, it was time for Bonnie to go home. She called her mom to come a pick her up.

By the time Bonnie's mom arrived it was almost 8 PM. After Bonnie and her mom left, LouAnn asked her mom if they could talk.

"Sure honey. What do you want to talk about?" asked her mom

LouAnn began, "It seems like every day you always yell and scream at me for one reason or another. It seems like you never talk to me or act like you did yesterday and today. Was this because Bonnie was here and I haven't had any sleepovers before? There have been times when I just want to stay in my room and hide, so I don't have to listen to you yelling. And then there are times, like last weekend, when you ask me about my school work or the book I was reading and it sounded as if you were interested. But then you wouldn't continue once I told you about it."

"Oh honey." her mom said, almost apologetic. "The other night your dad asked me why I always shouted and yelled at you when I wanted you or wanted you to do something.

Until then, I didn't realize I was even doing that. So, that night dad and I sat down and talked about how we have treated you and how bad we felt. He was even sorry for always watching TV during dinner and not paying any attention to you. We both love you very much. Please forgive us for the way we have been treating you."

Smiling, LouAnn said, "Of course I forgive you and dad. I love you both very much." With that, LouAnn got up and gave her mom a big hug and kiss. "It's getting late and I have a big day at school tomorrow, so I am going to head to my room and get some sleep. See you in the morning"

LouAnn's dream that night was the same as the night before, Hopper was talking to JJ.

# Chapter VIII

As LouAnn got up, she started thinking about talking with Miss Spaulding after school. Then it came to her that she had to face those girls again and deal with their bullying during the day.

*I've been dealing with them every day for a while, so another day will be no surprise.* She thought.

Bonnie was waiting for her outside the school. "Well, today's the big day. We get to see what Miss Spaulding has to say to us. Maybe she yelled at the girls and told them that if they didn't leave us alone, they would get suspended or something like that," said Bonnie.

"I am getting to that point where I really don't care anymore. I will just deal with it during the day and go home and try to forget about it. Oh, by the way how do you like my makeup? I decided to try it today and see how I like it all day," stated LouAnn.

Bonnie smiled and said, "I really like it on you. You look so different and so much better."

As they entered the school, they saw the girls standing by the lockers. As they passed the girls, they noticed the strange looks they were getting. The looks were more looks of surprise than anything else.

As the day progressed, LouAnn and Bonnie both noticed that many of the boys and other girls kept whispering as they saw the two friends walking the halls or in the cafeteria.

No-one made any nasty comments or bullying during the entire day, not even during lunch.

LouAnn looked up at the clock during her final class and noticed the bell was just about to ring. She now had to go to the cafeteria with Bonnie and see Miss Spaulding.

Seeing Bonnie in the hallway near the cafeteria, LouAnn said, "Well this is it. Let's hope that whatever Miss Spaulding has to tell us is good.”

As they entered the cafeteria, they were shocked to see Miss Spaulding and the girls. They thought they were only going to talk to Miss Spaulding.

“What are they doing here?” Bonnie asked Miss Spaulding as they got to the table. “We thought you were going to talk to just us.”

“I never said who was going to be here. All I said was that I had talked to these girls and wanted to see you this afternoon,” replied Miss Spaulding. “So let’s get started. LouAnn, would you please tell these girls why you say they are bullying and teasing you all the time.”

“Well,” said LouAnn nervously. “I have no figure, I am plain looking and, except for Bonnie, I have no friends. Even the boys tease me about how plain and boring I look. These girls are all so pretty and have figures already and are wearing bras. I’m not. I am not pretty like them. They even made comments about Bonnie when she started here at school because she was my friend.”

"OK, girls, now I want you all to tell LouAnn and Bonnie why you have been bullying and them," said Miss Spaulding.

Mattie, the one who seemed to be the biggest bully started. "It has nothing to do with how you look or the fact that you have no figure. We just used those words as an excuse because we knew that would get to you. The reason we have been treating you the way we have is because you are so smart. You get all A's in your classes and the teachers want you to help them a lot of the time. You are even in a couple of advance classes. We are jealous because we have a hard time in many of our classes and are lucky if get passing grades. Even the boys have told us about how smart you are. They are jealous too. So you see, it has nothing to do with your looks or your figure. Heck, my sister is older than us and she hardly has a figure. My mom said she is just a late bloomer. Miss Spaulding told us last week that she too, was a late bloomer. By the way, you look beautiful with makeup on. We think you should wear makeup all the time."

"So you can see what the girls are saying is so different from why you thought they were bullying you. All of you need to remember that it's what on the inside that matters not what you look like on the outside. Now, LouAnn and Bonnie, you have a choice to make. You can either forgive the girls and possibly become friends or just let things stay the way they are," said Miss Spaulding.

Looking at Bonnie, LouAnn said, "You have hurt me for a long time, but I will forgive you and, if you want try to become friends, I will give you a chance. I would even be willing to help each of you with your classes if you want me to. But, if this is some kind mean joke just because Miss Spaulding is here, then next time, I will go to the principal."

"No, we mean it. We are not just saying it. I, for one, would really like it if you would help me with my classes. I will also talk to all the boys and get them to stop teasing you. I will let them know that we were all wrong and that it was a big misunderstanding," replied Mattie.

LouAnn and Bonnie got up and went over and hugged the girls. They all smiled and walked off together talking.

*I can see they are going to get along great,* thought Miss Spaulding.

"Have fun as you all begin new friendships," shouted Miss Spaulding, as the girls were leaving the cafeteria.

Outside the school, Bonnie turned to LouAnn, "That was totally different than what I thought was going to happen. I like what you said and how you even offered to help them with their school work."

"Me too, but I'm really glad it worked the way it did. I learned that you always have to hear what the others have to say and not judge them first because their reasons my not be the reasons you thought." answered LouAnn. "I have to head home. Mom is going to give me a cooking lesson. See you tomorrow."

That night was a completely different kind of night at LouAnn's house. No screaming or yelling. Even dad was talking at the dinner table and not watching the game on TV. Before she knew it, it was 10 o'clock and she was tired after a long day.

She couldn't have been asleep more than 10-15 minutes before her birds showed up. When JJ flew in, the three young birds leaned away and puffed up their feathers. Hopper could tell they were scared—and so could JJ. The mock-ingbird perched himself on the opposite side of the old painted bunting.

"JJ what do you want to say to Joy, Grace, and Peanut?" asked Hopper.

JJ took a deep breath, and said, "I'm sorry for being mean—especially to you, Joy. I was jealous because you have friends, and I don't. I thought no one liked me because I'm big and not a pretty color like all of you. I thought that if you were all afraid of me, no one would know how sad I am to be alone. I know you talk behind my back, and it made me feel even worse."

"We never talked about you before you started bullying everyone," Peanut told him. "It's how you acted, not how you looked, that made us afraid of you and hide from you."

"I didn't know there was another way until I thought about what Mr. Hopper said," JJ explained. "Will you forgive me? I'm really sorry."

"What you said was mean and hurtful, and pulling my feathers hurt a lot," Joy said, still angry.

Grace chimed in, "What's changed, JJ? What made you decide to be nice to us?"

"I realized that if I want to have friends, I have to change the way I act and stop being jealous. Saying sorry doesn't mean much right now, but if you give me a chance, I will prove that I can be a good friend."

Hopper chirped, "What JJ is saying might be hard to accept, but give him a chance to prove that what he is saying is true."

Peanut, Grace, and Joy looked at one another, and, one by one, they nodded their heads in agreement.

Joy spoke on behalf of them all, "We'll give you a chance, but if this is some mean joke, we'll tell our parents and yours about what you've been doing."

Hopper flapped his wings. "JJ it's now up to you to keep your promise."

"I will!" JJ exclaimed, a little choked up. "Can we start now? I'll go get us something to share! Is everyone hungry?"

Naturally, they were all hungry, and so JJ was off and out of the barn, looking for a some-thing they could a share. A few minutes later, he was back with a plump juicy com cob from the corn field just outside the barn. The mock-ingbird's size certainly came in handy for more than just being a bully!

"This looks like the start of a great friend-ship," Hopper said happily. "Always remember, it's what's on the inside that matters. Look in-side yourself for the great friend you can be, not only to each other, but also to yourself."

With that, the five birds shared the corn cob, chirping between bites and getting to know one another.

There was even enough corn cob to go around for all of them to have seconds.

Once there wasn't a morsel left, Hopper flew back to his perch in the old red barn for a rest.

"Have fun flying together!" he called out, as the four friends took off in search of fun, new adventures.

LouAnn woke up smiling. Her dream about the birds ended just like it ended for her. She realized that she was meant to have that dream to show her how much better it is to talk things out and not keep it all tied up inside.

She couldn't wait to get to school and tell Bonnie how the dream ended.

At lunch, LouAnn and Bonnie sat with the other girls and LouAnn spent the entire time telling them about her dream and how it was very much like what was happening to her and how both her dreams and her real life problems ended so happily.

It is important that no matter how rough or bad you may think things are, there is always an answer, but you need to talk to someone about it.

# Chapter VIII

www.ingramcontent.com/pod-product-compliance
Lightning Source LLC
Chambersburg PA
CBHW070918160726
48004CB00003B/1413